The Asahel Curtis Sampler

Photographs of Puget Sound Past

edited by   David Sucher
foreword by   Murray Morgan
afterword by   Wes Uhlman

Puget Sound Access 1973 Seattle

Acknowledgements

I wish to thank the following people for their tremendous aid: Mr. Robert D. Monroe, Head, Photography Collection, Special Collections Division, University of Washington Library; Ms. Claudia Denney; Mr. Andrew Johnson, Librarian, Northwest Collection, Special Collections Division, University of Washington Library; Mr. Frank L. Green, Librarian, Washington State Historical Society; Mr. Jack Doughty and Mr. Archie Satterfield, of the Seattle Post-Intelligencer; Mr. Harvey Manning; Ms. C. J. Smith; Ms. Karyl Winn, Curator of Manuscripts, University of Washington Library; Mr. Steve Herold, Gritty Ink Scriptorium; Ms. Olga Stiffler.

Photographs

Photographs are courtesy of the University of Washington Library, Seattle, and the Washington State Historical Society, Tacoma.

Dates

Unfortunately, I have not been able to determine from external information the precise date (or in some cases, the place) of many of these pictures. However, with few exceptions the photographs are from the period 1900-1915.

The Future

Puget Sound Access is concerned about the future of the Puget Sound region and is working on books that deal with other aspects of life in the region. Furthermore, we would welcome any suggestions you have on other information events (books, posters, films, conferences, fairs, etc.) that can help us use our heritage with more intelligence.

Puget Sound Access
Box 4100
Pioneer Square Station
Seattle, Washington 98104

Printed in Snohomish, Washington by Sno-Graphics

Foreword

During the quarter century that I've been writing books about the Pacific Northwest, I've had the benefit of a secret weapon, almost an arsenal -- the Washington State Historical Society's collection of photographs by Asahel Curtis. When I've needed to get the feel of some area in the Northwest during the first thirty years of the 20th Century, my solution often has been to go to the library of the Ferry Museum overlooking the Stadium Bowl in Tacoma, and consult the Curtis albums.

In his old age, Asahel Curtis assembled a pictorial history of the Pacific Northwest, which he laid out in a dozen outsized albums for which he made some superb prints. Not all of the pictures are his own; like many photographers of his period he borrowed often and gave credit sparingly. The history contains, including the lifted items, only about 500 prints. The richness of the Curtis collection lies in the boxes of negatives -- nearly 60,000 exposures, and in the fading prints which Curtis pasted into old-fashioned, shoe-string tied photo albums. These are haphazardly assembled, sketchily identified, and many of his pictures are fuzzy and poorly composed. But they add up to an exceptionally complete record of the impact of the twentieth century on the frontier northwest.

Asahel Curtis neither won nor deserved the international reputation of his brother Edward. The brothers came to Seattle as teenagers in 1887, took up glass-plate photography as a hobby, and on the death of their father in the early 1890's turned professional. Both were ambitious, both talented, but Edward was touched with luck and genius. His early work brought him to the attention of prominent personages; Theodore Roosevelt gave him an introduction to J. Pierpont Morgan, and Morgan became the angel for Edward's magnificent twenty-volume study of the North American Indian -- a work gaining a second burst of popularity now that the copyrights are expiring and his pictures can be reproduced without tribute of royalties.

While Edward found a great theme in the American Indian, Asahel found an occupation in Amercian boosterism. His work was sponsored by chambers of commerce, boards of trade, industrial associations, promoters. He did not sell out: he believed in what he was doing. He loved the outdoors, but promoters-fashion: let's develop it. He was an apostle of Progress. That there might not be enough outdoors to go round was a concept foreign to Curtis and most of his contemporaries. His assignments carried him throughout the greater Northwest, to Alaska and British Columbia and the Yukon Territory as well as Washington, Oregon and Idaho. Wherever he went he shot pictures with the abandon of a journalist on expense account.

Edward was an artist, Asahel an artisan. Asahel did not specialize in Indians, though he took many Indian pictures. He was more interested in Process, in the growth of towns, the cultivation of crops, the fabrication of productions.

Edward composed his Indian pictures with the forethought of a sculptor. He claimed to have waited three years to get precisely the desired atmospherics for a shot of three chiefs on horseback under a brooding sky. He carried with him a considerable paraphernalia of wigs and artifacts in case the Indians he was to portray weren't authentic enough. Asahel settled for what the day offered. He was a legman getting the raw facts.

Both men photographed the Makahs. Edward arranged the Indians in harmonious compositions; Asahel caught them in disarray. In Edward's pictures every detail played a part in achieving the photographer's preconceived desire; in Asahel's pictures the dissarray was essential. The debris outside a Makah house, the whale skeletons and old boats and broken harpoons were part of Indian life, a boast of past wealth. They do not appear in Edward's neat arrangements; they are omnipresent in Asahel's. One brother photographed a white man's romantic dream of the Indian past; the other showed what a changing culture looked like at the moment of his visit. Asahel did not rearrange, he recorded. He was a good reporter.

I owe a great debt to the enormous file of Curtis prints at the State Historical Society Museum and to the smaller, but better printed collection at the University of Washington. The Asahel Curtis pictures have been under-publicized. Now they have been discovered by David Sucher, who in this album offers an intriguing sample of Asahel's work, garnished with quotations from contemporary publications which provide a quick study of the popular attitude in the Curtis era. I hope this sampler will lead to even wider use of the legacy left us by one of the most durable and indefatigable recorders of the Pacific Northwest, Asahel Curtis.

Murray Morgan

Introduction

While this book is by no means a biography of Asahel Curtis — and indeed this is not even a biographical essay — some words should be said about the man whose work we are sampling.

Seattle in the 1890's saw two brothers named Curtis start their photographic careers.

Edward S., the elder brother, has long been recognized as one of the great photographers of the early 20th Century. From the very start of his career his purpose was to chronicle the way of life of the American Indian. These first and most native of Americans he photographed as the "noble savage." Through his friendship with men of power, such as Theodore Roosevelt and J. Pierpoint Morgan, he gained the resources to travel North America to photograph peoples whose ancestral way of life was virtually gone. His photographs were brought together in a sumptuous twenty-volume series of books on the native peoples of North America, tribal group by tribal group. He was indeed a great photographer who was able to execute in a coherent manner a project of grand dimensions.

Asahel (1874—1941), the younger brother, was an equally fine craftsman who, because he pursued a more prosaic theme, has not received the attention he deserves.

Born in Minnesota and raised in Port Orchard, Washington, Asahel started his career in 1894 in Seattle and worked here steadily until his death, with only a few years away in San Francisco, the Yukon and Alaska in the late nineties. He was a homebody. While Edward traveled the continent, dined with Presidents and pursued the images of romantic hunters, Asahel stayed in Seattle and attended to his career.

Asahel Curtis was a Republican, active in Chamber of Commerce affairs, and throughout his life identified with the "economic interests" of his city. One looks in vain in his voluminous correspondence for any mention of art or culture or politics or even the broader ramifications of economic development, much less his own craft of photography. The only time he mentions photography is when he is asking a client about services needed, most often for a promotional brochure, which is not surprising.

After all, he was a "commercial" photographer, taking pictures of the products, processes and prospects of his region. His letters are full of admonitions and suggestions. He writes about improving the roads of the state, about the resolution of a conflict between several local dairies, about Seattle's need for water for industrial expansion, about the irrigation of Eastern Washington, about the building of a tramway to the top of Mt. Rainier, but never——or hardly ever in 30 years of letters——a word about the broader course of history in which he took so very active a part. And certainly never a word about photography.

He was widely known in his society, and his pictures were extensively used in advertisements, in local magazines such as ARGUS, SUNSET and THE COAST, and in national ones such as NATIONAL GEOGRAPHIC. He was particularly well-known for his mountain photography. Indeed, he was a founder of the Seattle Mountaineers——one of America's foremost climbing clubs——and made not a few "first ascents." In fact, he was the first professional guide on Mount Rainier. Yet, in a world that knows color photography, his scenes of timeless mountains are not so special. It is his commercial work that is most rewarding for they show people at work, interacting with the environment and with each other.

The Pacific Northwest——and Puget Sound in particular——is unique in the United States and perhaps the world, for its development was relatively late in the history of industrial expansion. Seattle was not founded until the early 1850's. Fortuituously, then, it is one of those rare places whose development from wilderness to metropolis has taken place in the photo age. The development of photography and the development of Puget Sound were simultaneous and, thus, we have an excellent record of the region from the time its native inhabitants were pushed out until its development as a major urban center. Here we can see how Edward and Asahel were a study in contrasts, Edward recording the decline of neolithic hunting cultures, Asahel the rise of an urban-industrial one. Both used photography as a tool: Edward the anthropologist, Asahel the "regional booster" who used photography as a tool to help the economic development of the State of Washington.

Curtis documented the development of the industrial ecology of Puget Sound and, thus, gives us a picture of a world whose problems we inherit. Remarkably, furthermore, not only did he "record", but his pictures were used as tools to encourage further development. He went beyond observation into participation and, therefore, foreshadows the "political photography" of today, which is designed not to be "pretty" but to tell a story, and by the telling of that story, move people to action. His pictures therefore can be seen as political tools.

Curtis was a "booster" and had attitudes that are important for us to understand. He was a man of his era and though he did think about the future, it was only as a straight-line projection of the present, and it all centered on the goddess "Growth" and how to entice her to the Pacific Northwest. He was a man who would and did write to the Mayor of Seattle and suggest, for instance, that a thorough study of the region's water resources was needed because otherwise there might be a scarcity that would hinder growth. However, his consciousness did not extend to envisioning a world where "growth" would not be courted but shooed. He was no environmentalist.

Though at personal level he enjoyed the outdoors, he put economic growth ahead of other kinds of growth. For example, he fought against expanding Olympic National Park and could say in 1933 that:

"Personally, I have always favored the building of a road through the Olympic Range. I know that there will always be plenty of wilderness left after all possible roads are built."

Perhaps the following passage will sum up his booster point of view:

The Spokane Spokesman-Review prints serious reflections on the plan of a Spokane citizen to overcome what we called the "depression", before the American Newspaper Publishers' Association deleted the word from newspaper vocabulary.

The Spokane genius would have the government issue twelve billion dollars in bonds, the major part of whose proceeds would be used to "excavate a huge incline tunnel into the earth's interior, penetrating as far as engineering, mechanical and scientific means will permit, using the excavated material for the construction of a huge science monolith, staggering in proportions — all nations invited to participate therein and to depict on the monolith's walls and interior the life and character of every people."

Our Spokane contemporary gently pooh-poohs the idea. But has it heard of the scheme of Asahel Curtis and Associates of Seattle? The scheme of Asahel Curtis & Associates also has to do with ending their here — er — deleted depression, but the money used in the enterprise would all be spent right in our midst, and for the story of Seattle.

Mr. Curtis and his collaborators would ask for only ten millions. Not $13,000,000; just $10,000,000. The money would be used to divert, by means of dams and great canals, all the waters of the Columbia River north of the Snake across the State of Washington. The river would be carried through the Cascade Mountains by a vast tunnel and emptied into Puget Sound.

This, says Mr. Curtis, somewhat bitterly, would make Portland the inland city that the Creator intended it to be.

Fully two billion horsepower in hydro-electric energy would be developed by the enterprise, and enormous electric fans would be installed in the tunnel. These fans would suck the moist air from Puget Sound and scatter it over the inland empire, thus making irrigation unnecessary. If the farmers refused to pay for the rain — and, of course, the scheme must be self-supporting — the fans would be turned the other way. Though the hot air of Eastern Washington would be distributed over Seattle, Seattle, as Mr. Curtis brightly remarks, is used to hot air.

The fruit orchards of the Yakima Valley would thereafter be grown on steel barges, using a syphoning method for irrigation. The barges at harvest time would be moored alongside docks and warehouses equipped with electrical picking and packing machinery and the fruit would go to market without the pollution of human hands.

Part of the material excavated from the tunnel would necessarily be dumped in Puget Sound and the Sound would be filled up south of Seattle, thus removing Tacoma from its position as competing port. But to compensate Tacoma, the remainder of the material would be built into a mountain on Stellacoom plains as big as Rainier — Tacoma could name it anything she wanted to.

All this could be done, conservatively, for ten million dollars, and in the process of construction employment could be found for everybody.

We rather suspect Asahel Curtis & Associates of spoofing the twenty-five million dollar highway-railway tunnel through the Cascades, the Hearst five billion dollar unemployment relief program and perhaps other schemes for making Uncle Sam the financial angel for this, that and the other scheme of enormous proportions. But sometimes a little spoofing takes the glitter off the unattainable."

During Curtis' life, the laboring classes were challenging the capitalists for a greater share in the wealth of society. The only way in this region— and in any other for that matter— that the titans could maintain political control was to raise the wages of their workers. The only way to do this was to make sure that the economy was constantly growing, for they certainly weren't going to give up their yachts and estates, and it was only a constantly expanding economy that could afford to increase wages to people at the bottom. It was a basic axiom of all the region's people that growth was good and the more growth the better; all political factions could at least agree on the goodness of growth.

To be a good commercial photographer one has to have an eye for the cultural images to which your audience will respond. Since Curtis' main goal was to show the advantages of life in Washington, his pictures show people——ordinary people, for the most part—— at work, in the street, in the field and factory, and, to a certain extent, at play. Everywhere he shows us activity, building and progress, alongside the "good life" of leisure for which Washington was famous even then.

*   *   *

It is commonplace nowadays that the growth of population, with concurrent growth of industrial and individual demands upon the natural systems of the region, are basic to the ecological crisis. Since Washington by current trends is not at the peak of its population growth, it behooves us to examine the process by which this growth has occurred. Encouragement of industrial and population growth has not been haphazard or accidental. The men who built this region understood quite well the relationship of their wealth to the size of the society which they ruled.

It is to a greater understanding of regional growth that this book is partially aimed, and it is my hope that the spirit of Asahel Curtis, a man who loved this region after his own fashion, will come through.

David Sucher

And now, you nature lovers; you open air cranks; you who are beginning to understand the care-free if deplorable independence of the hobo; you who marvel that there are so many beautiful things at your very doors you have never appreciated; you to whom the pungent ozone of piney woods or the humid tang of the surf means enjoyment beyond expression; you who thrill at the rhythmic hum of pistons and valves and cams and gears; to all you picture demons, speed fiends, Romanies of the road; to the rapidly increasing number of Americans who are beginning to appreciate America,

Greetings!

The Photomobile Tourist
1919

On the flanks of Mt. Rainier

First Americans

Makahs carving up a whale

The whale is landed on the highest place possible on the beach as well as convenient to haul away the remains of the carcass, for it emits a rank odor when the elements have busied on it for a short time .. . When the tide recedes, all hands entitled to a share swarm around the carcass with long, thick-bladed butcher knives and begin the butchering, stripping it off in blocks mostly two feet square. A sacred part forms the saddle, and the most choice part is taken from the head and is always the property of the hunter who pierced his harpoon in the whale, if he killed it alone. The other portions are divided and distributed proportionally according to an established rule, so that each one knows just exactly the quantity of whale blubber or meat he is to receive. This is a merry and joyous time .. . There is hardly any part of the whale that is useless to them. The blubber and flesh serve for food; the sinews are prepared and made into ropes and cords and used on various manufactures; the bladder and intestines are used for holding oil; and the bones and teeth utilized in fishing gear or curios. Of late years, the whales have not been so plentiful near the shore as in the past.

From four to ten of these huge leviathans are killed every year.

Seattle Post-Intelligencer
February 18, 1906

Indian Joe

From the earliest: Land use...

I am frequently in receipt of letters of inquiry concerning tide prairie——the practicability of reclaiming, the manner of dyking, culture, etc.; and I now have before me a letter from L.D. Andrews, of Seattle, in which he says:

"Many persons in Thurston and adjacent counties are making inquiries concerning the tidelands of the down Sound country, their location, extent, cost of reclaiming, productiveness, etc., and knowing that you have instituted a series of experiments with this kind of land, I beg of you as a favor and for the general interest of the Territory to give the public the benefit of your experiments and information in relation thereto through the columns of the Olympia *Transcript.*"

The above is the only apology I offer for the following essay, on a subject which, for many of your readers, needs no apology:

About four years ago, while on an excursion down-Sound, my mind was forcibly impressed with the extent, native verdure and beauty of the tide prairies, which environ almost every bay and borders every stream emptying into "that wonderful wilderness of water," as a San Francisco editor recently called our beautiful inland sea. The fact that no attempt had ever been made to reclaim these lands seemed the more strange, as they always lay immediately on the Sound, or the mouths of rivers, while settlements were formed fifty and sixty miles from ship navigation, and some hewn out of dense forests of timber. Knowing that in some European countries, and especially in Holland, this class of lands had been reclaimed at an immense cost, some of the dykes being thirty and even sixty feet high, and were more productive than any other, I became satisfied that our tide prairies, which never overflow more than a few feet at most, would pay well for the outlay necessary to bring them into a high state of cultivation. Accordingly, I resolved on the experiment, and settled on a piece of tide land at the mouth of the Snohomish River. But never having seen or read of a dyke in my life, I deemed it prudent to experiment with a few acres only, at first, and employed a man to dyke in three acres. According to the best information I could obtain, the tides never flowed these lands deeper than eighteen inches. The dyke was built 2½ feet high, and 4 feet on the base. It was complete in the Spring of 1864, but not in time to plant a crop that Spring. The following Winter's tides came through the earth wall about as freely as if it had been constructed of loose bricks. This was owing to the dyke having been thrown up without being packed, the subsoil being clay dried in chunks as it left the space.

In the Spring of 1866, I had one acre spaced two feet deep, the top soil turned in the bottom, and fruit trees planted; a variety of vegetables were also grown——cabbage with moderate success, turnips excellent, potatoes poor, peas grew and bore astonishingly well, tomatoes grew well and surprised every one who saw them by ripening well, strawberries seemed delighted with the soil, King Philip corn made good sized ears and filled well, but we gave it no opportunity to ripen, it was too tempting for the table. I planted a few rows of mangel-worzels, and these astonished the "oldest inhabitant." Not being acquainted with the habit of the "critter," I left them standing about six inches apart in the rows; they met, quarreled and elbowed each other about, until one-half were crowded out of the rows and half out of the ground. The largest were one foot in diameter and nearly three feet long. Asparagus grew moderately well, not as well as expected. Squashes grew, but not well. I experimented with grapes and cereals on a small scale; sowed two acres to timothy and red-top, without plowing, on land which had been tramped all Winter by cattle, and in July cut two tons per acre of excellent hay, but the greater part of it was native blue-grass,

which was in the ground before dyking, but had attracted but little attention; the heaviest crop of indiginous grass being red-top. It was soft and fragrant when cured, and cattle prefer it to timothy. Red clover which had been sown on spaded ground grew to the height of four feet the first season, and yielded three fine crops the second. I sowed some small native clover seed which came up, timidly, struggled a few months for existence and died. Barley ripened well, with large heads of grain. Spring wheat grew well, with very large heads of grain, twice as large as the seed sown. Oats grew luxuriantly, but kept on growing all fall and in fact nearly all winter, not more than one-half the grain getting ripe. The apple trees made but little new wood; plum trees made more; cherry trees grew about six inches, but a couple rows of pear trees made up for this delinquency by shooting up several feet.

Being now well satisfied that tide land would "pay" for dyking, if the dykes were properly constructed at first, I gave a contract for enclosing fifty acres, which was completed in the Fall of 1867. The dyke was two feet high, with a base of six feet. But the high tides of December, 1867, the highest ever known on the Sound, and which were three feet on the land, smashed the dykes into *pi* and burst open the sloughs, which had been timbered and filled with earth. The dyke around the house was broken also, but this was repaired immediately on subsiding of the water, which did no injury to the land. I had the dyke around this piece built four feet high, and it has not since been injured. Last season the apples grew as well as trees on up-land. I drilled several rows of rhubarb seed; the stems were over one inch in diameter, and the leaves attained the enormous width of two feet the first season. I experimented with onions also, and it was unanimously conceded that I had the finest crop that ever had been grown in the country. These grew on sod land, turned one spade deep the same day the seed was sown. Potatoes improve in size and quality as the ground is worked. Last year they were of ordinary size. I am satisfied the ground was spaded too deep for potatoes to do well the first season. I have been thus minute, at the risk of being tedious, because I could no other way give so correct an idea of the capabilities of the soil under consideration.

Persons desiring to locate tide lands will find the largest bodies at the mouths of the Snohomish, Statukahomish, Skagit, Samish, Nentsack and Lummi Rivers, and bordering the Swinimish Slough. The Swinimish prairies are said to be the finest and most extensive, containing ten or twelve thousand acres. The other tracts contain from four to five thousand acres each. The Lummi River, not marked on Mr. Giddings' late map, is said to have some excellent high grass prairies, in bodies of from three to five hundred acres, which are unsettled. The Snohomish prairies are considerably cut up with sloughs, but for grass and stock-raising purposes these are no disadvantage, as they form natural drainage which would otherwise have to be made.

Should the foregoing information give an impulse to the settlement of these hereto neglected but invaluable lands, I will consider myself amply compensated for this hastily written sketch. Should any person desire information concerning the method of constructing tide-gates, or building dykes, etc., and will address me by mail, I will furnish them with such as my experience has given me.

H.A. Smith, M.D.
Snohomish, W.T.
March 5, 1868

Dr. Smith of Smith's Cove, the present site of Piers 90-91

There never was a time in the history of Seattle when the realty market was so healthy and vigorous as it is this very moment. The boom days of 1890 are not in comparison at all, because the market of that period was altogether of the speculative quality, abnormal rather than normal, and therefore not healthy. The activity then prevalent was the feverish excitement that accompanies speculation on a large scale. The sales now are for homes and business purposes, every one of them adding to the permanent upbuilding of the city.

This movement must continue. Commercial centers do not reach the limit of growth and there stop, but expand indefinitely, in keeping with the ever-swelling tide of immigration, the natural increase of the world's population, and the growing wants of mankind. That Seattle is a center of commerce, and soon to be one of the world's great emporiums, is clear to any man familiar with the history of commerical development and the rise of cities and nations.

The commerical belt that encircles the world is between the thirty-fifth and fifty-fifth parallels of north latitude. In this path are nine-tenths of the wealth, nineteen-twentieths of the commerce, and three-fifths of the population of the globe. Inventive genius resides there. The forces that rule all races have their seats there. The brain and muscle that have carried civilization to perfection have been the products of those latitudes.

Berlin, Liverpool, Philadelphia, New York, Chicago and the Twin Cities are some of the links forming this great chain of commerce that started from China five centuries ago and has steadily pushed northwestward until it now spans the American continent and is about to forge the last link across the Pacific. This chain is bound together by climatic conditions and the shorter circumference of the earth, and no artificial cause can divert its course. Seattle is the link at the western extremity of the new world that will bind and complete the chain after a growth of five centuries with the original link in the heart of China. It is the seaport that will control the commerce of the Pacific as New York controls that of the Atlantic. Five transcontinental railways now converge here, or are coming as fast as men and money can bring them; while trans-Pacific steamers of the most modern build and the largest size are now in the stocks to bridge the space between the Russian system of railways terminating at Port Arthur and Vladivostok and the American systems terminating at Seattle.

Before many years Alaska will contain as much population as Norway, Sweden, Denmark and Holland combined. Washington, Idaho, Montana and Oregon will eclipse other states of like area, for none equal these in the natural advantages of soil, minerals and climate. Seattle will be the geographical and commercial center of it all.

The City of Seattle
Seattle Chamber of Commerce
1900

A Seattle subdivision

The pleasing fact about all these towns is that every community itself takes its development in hand. It is not left to real estate agents. These men recognize the value of men and of industries to the whole community, and the whole community goes about the task of inducing men to go there. I have before me a thick and attractive, illustrated pamphlet about Snohomish County. The first half leaf in it is a postal card addressed to the Commercial Club of —— (you write the name of any town in the county about which you wish to get information), and on the back of the card this sentence is printed: "I want to know more about your town and county with a view to engaging in ---." If you sign your name and send that card, you will get information from a man who represents the public spirit of the whole town and who has no private bargain to drive with you.

The World's Work
August 1905

A factory

There is no land anywhere that should not be surrendered on call to industry. Industry gives the wherewithal to build homes where you will. The more industry the more homes, and the more beautiful. Opposition to providing all possible land for the development of the industrial side of the community is either blindness to opportunity or treason to the commonwealth.

The Town Crier
December 1910

The Lake Washington Drive, with Mt. Rainier in the distance

...The (Lake Washington) drive is not the primary purpose of the park. The park is a piece of landscape and the drive is merely the means of making these landscapes conveniently accessible and enjoyable by people in carriages and on foot...

Olmsted Brothers, 1904
Letter to the Seattle Park Board

...Port of Seattle!

Grave Orientals, big Norsemen from Bergen, gallant schooners from Alaska, maybe a barkentine from Australia and huge tramps from anywhere——from nowhere! Stately, rhythmic, unhurried and with profound dignity they enter the crescent-shaped harbor——five miles from tip to tip. It is a great, epic poem. To think that in a few years this Western city has jumped into foreign trade so eagerly that today it ranks third to New York and Boston in value of foreign imports. I couldn't believe this until I looked up the government reports.

These two hundred miles of waterfront, with their ordered dignity of piers and warehouses, wharves and cold storage, dry docks and custom houses——the large trafficking in an infinite range of commodities and the fascinating infinitude of commerce——hemp from India and Fordsons for Siam; rattan furniture from China and condensed milk for babies in Tokio; cotton for Japan exchanged for silk to be transhipped to Paterson, New Jersey. Spices and silk! And tea for all the afternoon teas in America. And lumber going out to rehabilitate Japan. Detroit automobiles for the Orient; apples for Europe; fresh loganberries, in ice, for London; and salmon for the world! Reindeer, shipped 2500 miles from Alaska in cold storage, and berries as well——there is no end to the romance of it. Then to see with seeing eyes——gray pier, jade water, architectural beauty of utility; the color and the endless activity of cranes and derricks and tractors, stevedores and Dane sailors and South Americans——romance, mystery, commerce——economics, product of the maritime craftsmanship of the ages—— self-consious, high-blazoned——"Port of Seattle."

Yet Seattle betrays herself no where as a manufacturing city — there is no particular manufacturing district — no prominence of smoke — because she is so geographically immense. It is as though one were to take the great congest of the Naugatuck Valley in Connecticut and spread it out; it would make industry, as it does in Seattle, almost pastoral. I have seen with my own eyes cows grazing in a pasture adjoining a tall, chimney-towered factory, both the factory and the cows appearing contented. It is destined that Seattle shall remain attractive despite her expansion. Manufacturing is zoned; the city has been planned; homes will ever be distinctive.

Which is typical of the potential breadth for expansion that is Seattle's. Already she has a wealth of manufactures, but she has the potentialities——for such a wealth of industry as only her bravest dream of. With a tremendous and truly terrible hydro- electric power waiting to be chained for use, with her pivotal position, tying America with the Orient, Siberia and Alaska, with a reserve of back-country fabulous in its possibilities——it must——Seattle must become an industrial colossus. Do we——dreamers and lovers and artists——wish it so? That is nothing. Would we wish a lovely girl to say so: No, Seattle must go to her great ultimate. It is the machine age. And she is already flirting boldly with her lover——Industry.

Seattle: Her Faults and Her Virtues
Almira Bailey
1925

Along Elliott Bay, the origin of Seattle's strength

Seeing Seattle

There is possibly no better method of gleaning an adequate idea of the beauties of Seattle's residence district than by a trip in the "Seeing Seattle" car of the Seattle Electric Co. There are two things which are necessary to make such a service a success. One is something to see and the other is somebody to see it. Seattle has always had the first. And that she has the second is demonstrated by the fact that during last summer there were times when it took eight large cars to accommodate the crowds of tourists who desired to make a trip over the city.

The car makes a loop through the business section of the city, passing the largest office buildings, wholesale and retail stores, hotels, etc.

It passes Pioneer Square, the site of Henry Yesler's saw mill in 1854, the first industry of importance to locate in Seattle. The Totem Pole was brought from an Indian village on Tongas Island, Alaska, by a businessmen's excursion some five years ago. It is estimated to be over one hundred years old and is one of the finest in existence. It is supposed to be the record or history of some tribe or family of Indians now extinct — a very unique family tree.

The next point of special interest is the Great Northern Docks, the home port of J. J. Hill's great trans-Pacific liners, the "Dakota" and "Minnesota," the largest steamers on the Pacific. These docks are also the American port of the "Nippon Yusen Kaisha" (Japan Mail Steamship Co.). This company, which is controlled entirely by Japanese capital, is one of the largest steamship corporations in the world, and its boats have been extensively used by the Japanese government as scout cruisers and transports during the war with Russia. Other boats loading at these docks carry American products to all parts of the world.

The car then reaches Ballard, which is soon to be annexed to Seattle. Population, 10,000. Largest shingle manufacturing town in the world, and the seat of many important and extensive lumber manufacturing industries.

Between Ballard and Fremont the car follows the route of the proposed ship canal, which is to connect Lakes Union and Washington with Puget Sound, thus giving Seattle a magnificent fresh water harbor. The estimated cost of the canal is $7,500,000.

Then comes Green Lake, the smallest of the three lakes in the city limits, being about three hundred acres in extent. The surrounding shores are thickly built up with comfortable homes, making this one of the city's most popular and attractive suburbs. The "Seeing Seattle" car loops Green Lake, passing through Woodland Park, a beautiful natural resort, the largest of the city's pleasure grounds.

Returning to the city proper from Green Lake, the car follows the shore of Lake Union for upwards of a mile. A number of small manufacturing enterprises are here located, and a distant view can be had of the buildings and grounds of the State University.

No visitor to Seattle should fail to visit Capitol Hill. This tract, now adorned with beautiful homes, is a typical example of Seattle's rapid growth; less than five years ago it was covered with a thick forest. Fortunes have been made in the last few years in real estate investment in this and other sections of the city.

Madrona Heights affords a magnificent view of Lake Washington, Mount Rainier, and the Cascade Range. In Lake Washington, which forms the city's eastern boundary, Seattle possesses an unrivaled attraction. This body of water, fed by mountain streams, is from one to four miles wide and twenty-eight miles long, never freezes, is navigable to steamers at all times of the year, and on the completion of the government canal it will probably be used as a naval base.

These are but a few of the attractions to be found on this trip, which, it is safe to say, for diversified scenery of mountain, lake, sound and city cannot be duplicated in the world.

The Argus
1905

Sight-seeing as it was done

Transportation: By land...

Leave Seattle for Tacoma, corner Occidental Avenue and Yesler Way, 6:30, 8, 9, 10, 11 AM and 12, 1, 2, 3, 4, 5, 6, 7, 8, 9, 10, and 11:30 PM. Trains leaving at 9:00 AM and 4:00 PM make no stops between Seattle and Tacoma. Time, one hour and fifteen minutes.

Raymer's Dictionary of Greater Seattle
1907

The Seattle-Tacoma Interurban

A car of Seattle's Madison Street Line

Seattle street car rides

Mineral and Sulphur Springs, Ravenna Park. Take Ravenna Park or Eastlake car on Third Avenue south of Union Street. Time of trip, 40 minutes.

Flower Gardens, conservatory, water tower observatory, at Volunteer Park. Take Capitol Hill car on Third Avenue south of Pine Street. Time, 30 minutes.

Zoological Gardens, at Woodlawn Park. Take Green Lake or Phinney Avenue car on Second Avenue, south of Pike Street. Time, 35 minutes.

Giant Fir and Cedar Trees at Schmitz Park. Take Alki Point car on First Avenue south of Virginia Street. Time of trip, 40 minutes.

Canoeing and lake steamboating at Leschi Park. Take First, Second, Third or Fourth Avenue cars going south and transfer to the Yesler cable line. Time of trip, 25 minutes. Boating and steamer rides at Madison Park also. Take Madison Park car on Third Avenue south of Pike Street or Madison cable line. Time of trip, 35 minutes.

Municipal Bathing Pavilion, Duwamish Head. Take Alki Point car on First Avenue going south. Time of trip, 40 minutes.

View of Mt. Rainier, Japanese Pagodas, Hanging Gardens, Lake Washington from Madrona Park. Take car on Broadway, bound south. Time, 30 minutes.

Bridle paths for pedestrians and saddle horses, Washington Park. Entrance, Madison and Thirty-first Avenue. Take Madison Park car.

University of Washington Campus, Formal Gardens, Open Air Theatre. Take Ravenna Park, Wallingford Avenue or Cowen Park cars on Third Avenue south of Union Street. Time, 35 minutes.

Government Fort and Barracks. Take Fort Lawton car on First Avenue. Military band concerts at designated times. Time of trip, 45 minutes.

Lumber and Shingle Mills at Ballard. Take Fremont-Ballard or Ballard Beach cars on First Avenue, north bound. Time, 40 minutes.

Fish Canneries, Ship Building Yards, Flouring Mills and other Seattle industries, along Railroad Avenue, south of Yesler Way. Take First Avenue South car.

Seattle: Residential Advantages and Attractions for Tourists
Oregon-Washington Railroad and Navigation Company
1914

...and Water

One of Joshua Green's boats

Shipbuilding at the Hall yard, Port Blakely

During the time the plant was located at Port Blakely 77 vessels were constructed, among them some of the finest schooners afloat . . . Many of the large schooners built under the supervision of Mr. Hall are known all over the world. They are magnificently built vessels, big carriers and good sailors. . . In building a vessel, Mr. Hall put in the best material that could be bought. In all his dealings he was as square as a die, a priceless heritage to leave behind.

Railroad and Marine News
December 1916

Gold

The establishment of a Government assay office in Seattle, according to the statements of prominent businessmen and members of the Chamber of Commerce, will mean as much or more for Seattle than the proposed smelter. From the Klondyke country alone it is estimated that $1,000,000 in gold dust and nuggets will reach Seattle this fall. Heretofore, the output of the Alaska mines has been carried on to the San Francisco mint simply because of no means of disposing of it here to any representative of the Government . . . The men who bring in the gold representing their summer's efforts in the mountains will not need to go to San Francisco to dispose of it. They will deposit the proceeds in the Seattle banks and will spend the money here.

The Seattle Daily Times
July 13, 1897

The excitement in this city became intense yesterday when through dispatches it was learned that Prof. T.S. Lippy had arrived in San Francisco with $65,000 in real yellow nuggets. Prof. Lippy is so well known here as to preclude all possibility of an exaggerated statement from him, and the result is that half of Seattle would like to go forthwith to the Klondyke and the other half objects strongly to staying at home. On every street corner, in every office and store, all along the waterfront, at police headquarters, and everywhere, nothing can be heard but Klondyke, Klondyke, Klondyke.

The Seattle Daily Times
July 16, 1897

Steamer Portland, from St. Michaels, arrived at the dock this morning, bringing miners from the far-famed Klondyke, having in their possession enough gold to almost startle the world and variously estimated at from half to a ton's weight.

The Seattle Daily Times
July 17, 1897

The history of the Klondyke rush is familiar to all. Inside of twenty-four hours half of the male population of this city had developed the fever for gold. Every available craft was pressed into service. Sturdy frontiersmen who had prospected from the Mississippi to the Coast and from Mexico to British Columbia rubbed elbows with men like former Governor McGraw and General E. M. Carr in an effort to reach the new El Dorado. Steamers, sailing vessels and scows in tow left for the north. Supplies became so short that prices soared upward.

In less than a week Seattle, which from the first was acknowledged to be the outfitting point for Alaska, was so crowded with Easterners that they frequently slept in the streets. The railroads were completely swamped with freight. Wholesale houses worked their crews day and night. Vacant stores, residences and offices filled up as if by magic. Men who had never seen six inches of ice outside of a refrigerator advertised new methods, which they had invented, for extracting the frost from the ground. A score of big steamships left the Eastern coast in a mad rush around Cape Horn in an effort to get in the game, and reap some of the reward.

The Argus
December 1913

Weighing the first shipment of gold

Getting ready for Alaska

There were many comic, as well as tragic, incidents connected with the Klondyke stampede. An Easterner, going North with his wife, had engaged a stateroom on the hurricane deck of one of the largest steamers. Came sailing day. The boat was crowded from stem to stern with freight, and at last it was necessary to put some cattle on the hurricane deck. There was absolutely no other place for them.

And then the Easterner rushed to the Captain.

"Look here," said he, "I paid a big price for a stateroom for myself and wife, and when I go to it I find a cow sticking her head through the window."

"I am very sorry sir," said the Captain, "but as you see we are so crowded that we have been compelled to put freight everywhere, and you will have to put up, I am afraid, with a little inconvenience. I will, however, do the best I can for you. John, go up on the hurricane deck and turn that cow around!"

The Argus
December 1913

This United States Government Institution in Seattle was created by Act of the United States Congress on the 21st of May, 1898, and opened for business on the 15th of July, following.

Seattle, being that port on the Pacific Coast from which depart and arrive fully three-fourths of all those going to and returning from the Klondike and Alaskan gold fields, it was self-evident that a United States Government Institution, for the purchase of placer gold and bullion, should be established in Seattle, so that the returning argonauts might dispose of their golden treasure without delay or further inconvenience.

How well this has been accomplished, a few figures will demonstrate. Since the Institution opened for business — July 15, 1898 — to the close of business on November 30, 1899, there were 8,209 individual deposits, carrying a value of $18,358,946.20, thus producing an average of considerably over $1,000,000 per month. This places the Institution first on the list of kindred institutions in the United States for volume of virgin placer gold handled and third in volume of business transacted. It is most assuredly a record of which every citizen of the State of Washington is proud.

The Institution is under the management of the Government appointee, the Hon. Frederick A. Wing, who is broad-minded in his views of conducting an institution established to aid in the development of the mineral resources of the great Pacific Northwest. It is under this able management that eighteen millions of dollars worth of gold dust have been purchased and accounted for to the Government without the loss of a cent or the occurrence of an incident to mar the efficiency or standing of the Institution.

Everything possible is done to accommodate each depositor. The gold dust is weighed in his presence and he can check the weight if he so desires. There is issued to him a negotiable receipt specifying the number of ounces of his deposit, so that he may at once obtain money from any of the Seattle banks. If he does not care for immediate funds, he can, under ordinary circumstances, call at the Assay Office the following day and receive a certificate showing in detail the value of his deposit, together with draft in full settlement. If he does not care for the money, his bar of gold will be delivered to him, with the certificate just mentioned, on payment of the regular Government charges — which are indeed very nominal, rarely covering cost of material used in determining value of the deposit. If he desires to leave the city immediately, it is arranged to remit the proceeds of his deposit to him. It is therefore quite plain that the wishes of practically every depositor can be fully met.

The Institution, having been established but a little over a year, its equipment is of the latest design that experience has proved practical. Instead of the slow going and unevenly distributed heat of the charcoal furnace for melting the gold, the Institution is equipped with the very latest and best gas furnaces. Likewise, in assaying, the most practical and up-to-date methods known to science, the most delicate balances and testing instruments are used. In fact, no antiquated materials, appliances or methods are a part or parcel of the Institution, and it is with pardonable pride that the people of Washington point to the Government Assay Office at Seattle as an institution vastly beneficial to the general interests of the commonwealth.

The City of Seattle
Seattle Chamber of Commerce
1900

Smelting gold in the Seattle assay office

Monte Cristo

Monte Cristo! Here the railroad can go no further. Huge mountains rear their exalted summit high into the heaven's ethereal blue. The place is surrounded by snowy crests and jagged peaks. On all sides one sees the great, high walls of rock and trees which rise to an altitude of over 7,000 feet... In addition to its great beauty of scenery, it is rich in mineral deposits and resources which as yet have scarcely been touched. The ore carries gold, silver, arsenic and iron...The place has a school, a gravity water works system, and is lighted by electricity from the mill. The town has a population of several hundred and is a typical and interesting mining camp. A fine, large hotel is located here with all modern conveniences.

The Coast
June 1903

The town of Monte Cristo (1902)

Avalanche!

Retrieving a body from the Wellington avalanche (1910)

Wellington, Saturday, March 13 —— If the Great Northern's information is complete, there are left in the Wellington avalanche but nine bodies. The estimated number of dead passengers and trainmen has been cut down to 89, and the eighth was taken from the ruins of train No. 35's day coach late last evening . . . Because there is yet a chance that the officials do not know of all who were on the doomed train the night of the slide, the search will not be given up when the last person on the present list of the missing is found.

"There is no way at present of telling positively when we have located all the bodies, 'said Borthwick tonight,' and for that reason I presume we shall be compelled to continue the search until the side of the hill is bared'.

The Seattle Times
March 3, 1910

Coal

Sorting coal at a mine east of Lake Washington

Coal mining is one of the leading industries of the State of Washington, and particularly of King County. The output of the coal mines average 3,000,000 tons annually, valued at about $9,000,000. The coal fields of Washington cover an area of several thousand square miles. The deposits of coal are practically inexhaustible and the quality is of the best for manufacturing, steam, and domestic use.

The coal on the west side of the Cascade Mountains will go to Seattle for consumption and shipment except so much as may be wanted for iron making and other manufacturing purposes along the line of the road. Coal will be in demand for furnaces, foundaries, engines, etc. in Seattle, Spokane Falls, and many other places. But its largest consumption will be in the iron furnaces which will be erected for smelting the ores of the Cascade Mountains.

A Report on Washington Territory
1889

Waiting to enter the mine

The Lake Washington Ship Canal

Before the Ship Canal: Portage Bay with Lake Washington in the background

A few years ago the dense fringe of forest encircled Lake Washington with scarcely a perceptible break. The bear, the deer, and their companions of the wood, came unmolested to drink on the beach, and the myriads of wild fowl were free from the possibility of fright at the puffing steamer. There was, perhaps here and there, a logger's camp or a pioneer's cabin, but, on the whole, it was a magnificent wilderness, and the signs of a great development were indeed few. Today, the scene is changed: the logging camps are more numerous and large lumber mills at different points are doing their share of the great lumber business of the Puget Sound region. Fruitful farms have been cleared about the pioneers' houses, and substantial residences have taken the place of the log cabins. Towns have come into existence and are growing rapidly, and to accommodate traffic, a score of steamers ply between the different points. And now, too, along the eastern shore is being rapidly pushed to completion a railway...known as the Lake Washington Belt Line. It will not be long before a ship canal from the Sound to the Lake will afford the way for ocean vessels to reach and meet the tracks of the railway on the shores of what will then be the finest fresh water harbor in the world...Following the completion of the canal, it is almost a certainty that, within a decade, there will grow up about the steel works now being built a manufacturing city that will rival in point of population and commercial wealth any of the larger manufacturing cities of the East——a city that will stretch for miles along the eastern shores of Lake Washington.

**Lake Washington and Kirkland: Commercial
Key of the Puget Sound Region**
Seattle
1891

Water joining water: Lake Washington being joined to Portage Bay

The Ship Canal project, when first conceived, was not based upon any immediate commercial need but was looked upon as a wise provision for the future commerce of the city. The time has now arrived, even sooner than its most sanguine advocates anticipated, when it is an **imperative necessity** for the accommodation of the commerce that is already assured. Two-thirds of the present salt waterfront of the city is now occupied by wharves, docks, and warehouses that are taxed to their utmost capacity, and growing at the rate at which our commerce is now growing and seems sure to grow hereafter, the whole waterfront will be overtaxed before the canal, even if built with all possible speed, could be completed.

Laborers with shovels cut away the narrow strip of earth holding back the waters of Lake Union at 2 o'clock yesterday afternoon, permitting 45,000,000 gallons of water to flow into the Portage cut, which now connects Lake Washington and Lake Union. In constantly widening stream, the waters ate into the cofferdam, and in a few minutes the flow was roaring with the sound of a cataract.

The whole effect was a lesson in the terrific effect of flood waters. When the men with their shovels had broken the narrow neck of land, they sprang aside just in time to escape the inflow of the water, which descended thirty-seven feet to the bottom of the cut. At first a tiny streamlet, the incoming water widened rapidly. In ten minutes the crowds on the cofferdam fled to escape being plunged into a raging torrent on the sides of the bank, which caved in in huge sections.

Letter from the Seattle Chamber of Commerce
  to the U.S. Army Board of Engineers
1902

The Seattle Post-Intelligencer
August 26, 1916

Reclaiming the Tidelands

Dearborn had one idea. It was with him always, to the exclusion of all other thoughts. The merits of this idea he set forth for twenty years, discoursing, rambling endlessly from breakfast till bedtime. Wherefore H. H. Dearborn became a bore. People fled at his approach. They knew what was coming. At the club, chairs became vacant and groups melted away when the old man began his inevitable refrain:

"Waal, friends, tide-lands has riz. Tidelands is bound to go higher. Better come over to the office and let me fix up a deed to a piece of it. It'll only cost you ten a month, and it'll make you a fortune. Yes, sir, tide-lands has riz."

Like croaking Cassandra in ancient Troy, Dearborn, the insistent mud-flat optimist of Seattle, became a town character. His slogan "Tide-lands has riz" became a by-word on the streets, but his message to the Trojans of Puget Sound fell upon ears as deaf as those that listened to the ancient seeress of woe. Only a few men, peering into the ooze at the mouth of Duwamish creek as into a crystal ball, shared Dearborn's vision of the big values buried in the mud. C. B. Bussell, having bought heavily in the prehistoric time before gold was discovered in Alaska, faithfully paid his taxes and joined in Dearborn's song. Victor Hugo Smith, a bank clerk of narrow means, weighted his savings and cast them into the upper end of Elliott bay, there to be covered by the rising tide. But the general public merely grinned, lifted the index-finger to its forehead significantly and went its way. Conservative firms hesitated when asked to list tide-lands. True, these lands had been officially platted by the state twenty-five years ago, deep slips had been laid out for the ships of the Seven Seas, the boundaries of land, water, of streets, railroad tracks, of docks and factory sites had been neatly indicated — on paper — but unfortunately the boundaries of streets and lots had to be marked by buoys instead of stakes, the entire tract being covered with water to a depth of five to thirty feet, according to the stage of the tide. Investors preferred to put their money where it could be found without a divine suit. They admitted all the premises of the mud-flat enthusiasts. They agreed that Seattle was bound to become a skookum big city, that the area of level land available for railroad yards, factories, shops and warehouses was rather limited, that eventually the odoriferous tide-lands would be needed for the terminals of the coming transcontinental roads, but nevertheless they declined to buy submarine real estate.

"Tide-lands has riz" chuckled Dearborn triumphantly in 1905.

The Puget Sound extension of the Milwaukee, needing terminals in Seattle, was buying tide-lands, but the purchases were spasmodic only. They lacked vigor, snap and continuity. Toward the end of 1905 the tide-land market had resumed its usual somnolent condition. However, the spurt had been sufficient to whet the appetites of the comparatively small group that owned the largest part of the amphibious real estate. They were sitting tight, hopeful, expectant, bound by a quiet little gentleman's agreement in restraint of tide-flat trade. They were to notify one another immediately of any new offer, that the pool's prices might be governed accordingly.

On the second day of January, A. D. 1906, the tide-land market was decidedly bearish, inactive, dull. Not even a wash sale was perpetrated. Upon the third day of January the bulls were rampant, bellowing for block after block of the submerged land. The Union Pacific, intent upon a foothold in the Puget Sound capital, was buying, buying, buying into the strategically most valuable portion of the tide-lands. Its sledge-hammer blows at last drove into Seattle's consciousness a realization of the tide-flats' full value. Three weeks after the opening of the railroad's short buying campaign, C. B. Bussell deposited a check calling for a cash payment of $395,000 in his bank. That money represented but a small part of his tide-land holdings. By the middle of February his cash balance had risen to $700,000. In H. H. Dearborn's office — "Tide-lands has riz," in poster type, was his trademark now — buyers were standing in line waiting for their turn. Smith, the bank clerk, quit counting other people's money; he was too busy with his own. Everybody was buying tide-lands; everybody able to scrape up a few hundred dollars expected to get rich overnight. When the short sharp buying campaign was over, Seattle had added a collection of tide-flat millionaires to the ranks of its six-cipher aristocracy. Some of them dropped out again in short order. Being men of one idea, their judgment on matters not related to tide-flats did not always prove sound, and a large part of their sudden wealth as suddenly reentered general circulation. But the tide-lands, rising out of the water as the tops of the hills were washed into them, justified the high values so spectacularly thrust upon them. Today, Seattle is preparing to spend many millions in their improvement that the expected rush of marine traffic from Panama to Puget Sound may be handled with efficiency and dispatch.

Sunset
July 1912

Filling the tidelands of Elliott Bay

About three years ago, Seattle became thumb-worn on the map through so many railroad presidents putting their finger upon the spot when talking expansion and extension to their associates. Both the Chicago, Milwaukee and St. Paul and the Union Pacific decided to build into Seattle. The only place where they could locate their terminals with convenience and profit was upon these tidelands. Naturally that created a boom in these lands. It is a well known fact that the most available sites for manufactures and all business more closely connected with railroads than with pedestrians is in the neighborhood of the railroad lines and especially of the railroad terminals. This fact created another demand as soon as the first fact became established.

It is not necessary to dwell in particular upon what happened. Even the few who have not already heard something of that remarkable real estate campaign in the midst of which two great railway companies poured million after million in money can at least imagine its possibilities. The men who reaped the fullest measure of the profit were old timers in Seattle who had refused to consider these mud flats a blemish upon the fair face of the city and had quietly and sincerely invested their money there long years before. These and a few of the more quickly awakened who were able to hear the first rumble of the approaching trains —— these are the tideland millionaires.

Sunset
November 1907

There is in existence a slang phrase which describes a certain class of men in Seattle and to a certain extent the phrase describes them truly and well. It describes them truly, when conditions are considered and when the real meaning of the phrase is understood. There are in Seattle what are known as tideland millionaires. It is the fashion among some to speak the phrase with a sneer and yet it includes some of the best and shrewdest business men in the city.

To understand it, one must realize at least a little bit of one of the greatest engineering feats ever attempted in this country and understand a little bit about one of the most remarkable commerical growths which any city has witnessed since the days when Chicago sprang out of a creek into a metropolitan life. Whatever of opprobrium may rightfully attach to the title rests solely upon the newness of the wealth which gives it license and not at all to the source from which it came. In a few cases, it was luck pure and simple which landed the favorite of fortune in this class, but in the great majority of cases it was far-sighted business policy. It was nerve backed with money at the right time and an abiding faith in the future of the city which caused the possessors of these attributes to success to be thus decorated in the city where they had planted their hopes and built their homes that they might await the harvest.

The tidelands are the broad delta of the Duwamish River, formed by the varying flow of the melting glaciers on the slopes of the Cascade Mountains. Prehistoric torrents upon their rush to the salt water in Elliott Bay has worn away the bluffs to the south of Seattle and created a broad flat over which the tide ebbed and flowed. Ten years ago it was merely an evil-smelling expanse of salt-flavored mud, and all but a few of the inhabitants swore whenever the wind blew from the southwest.

But some of those who didn't swear saw possibilities in that stretch of mud and some of those who saw invested their money in lands which were at times under fifteen or twenty feet of water. These saw that level ground was going to be the greatest commodity upon the market of the bigger and better city, which they had in the back of their heads, and they realized that this stretch of mud was to be the first and most available land to be seized upon when the time came.

Sunset
November 1907

Elliott Bay from the Centennial Mill (1902)

Regrading the Hills

Regrading a Seattle hill

Situated as it is on the western slope of a steep ridge and held in from western expansion by Puget Sound, Seattle has had much to overcome in laying out a city where business could be transacted with minimum traffic grades from one section to another.

With the enormous increase in manufacturing and commerce due to the Alaskan, Oriental and Coast trade, the influx of transcontinental carriers, and consequent development of other industries, Seattle has had to look for a larger business area, adjacent to her waterfront, and in doing this the city has perhaps met and overcome more impropitious obstacles than any other American city. This demand for increased space has been met by the carving of low gradient north and south throughfares along the side of the hill, the removing of immense natural barriers separating the northern and southern outlying districts from the business center, and the raising of the southern tide flat district to an elevation above high water.

New projects in which the cost of improvement amounts to 50 per cent or more of the assessed valuation of the property are put before the City Council in the form of a petition, which must be signed by at least 75 per cent of the interested property holders. When the proposition is passed upon, the City Engineer's office lays out the district and prepares an estimate of the cost of the improvement. This cost is proportioned to the private property according to frontage, and the owner has the option of paying cash or in yearly installments for a term of from five to ten years. The city then issues local improvement bonds to the amount of the estimate, which bear interest at six or seven per cent and are secured by a first lien on the property in the district. The cost of the improvement of the private property is paid to the contractor directly.

At the present time, operations are being carried on in three districts, viz., the Jackson Street, Denny Hill and Dearborn St. districts.

The Jackson St. et al. contract was awarded April 23, 1907, to Lewis & Wiley, Inc. at a unit cost of 10 cents per cubic yard for excavation and 15 cents per cubic yard for embankment. The district comprises 68 square blocks of property situated in the southern part of the city, being bounded by Washington Street on the north, Addition Street on the south, Fifth Avenue on the west, and Twelfth Avenue on the east.

The Argus
1909

Moving a house while regrading

The Denny Regrade in progress

DISCUSSIONS

Charles Evan Fowler,* M. Am. Soc. C. E. (by letter) — The regrading of Seattle, as carried out largely under R. H. Thomson, M. Am. Soc. C. E., and the author, approached in magnitude of the material to be handled, the digging of the Panama Canal, and in some respects the difficulties were much greater. The first extensive regrading was done by steam shovels on Denny Hill near the old Washington Hotel, and one on the old University grounds on Fourth Avenue. The material was sold to the Great Northern Railway for tide-flat filling.

The steam shovels were served by horse-drawn, 2½-yd. dump wagons, from 24 to 30 for each shovel, and the dirt was hauled about ½ mile to the north end of the Great Northern Railway Tunnel, where it was chuted into railway dump cars about 30 ft. below, and hauled in trains to the final place of deposit, south of the Great Northern Station. The selling price was 7 cents per cu. yd., which, added to the excavation price, made the total receipts about 20 cents per cu. yd., or a very profitable figure for the pre-war period.

The dumping grounds were just south of the territory and comprised several hundred of the 1200 acres of the Seattle tide flats, which were brought to grade at 2 ft. above extreme high tide. This filling was done by the writer with two 20-in. hydraulic dredges, and the 12,000,000 cu. yd., so placed, formed an essential part of the regrade work of Seattle, making usable the land from the foot of Queen Anne Hill to the southern end of Elliott Bay. The portion of the tide flats near the Jackson Street regrade was filled with the dirt sluiced down in doing this work. This, together with the material removed from the Denny Hill regrade, constitutes the greatest sluicing operation ever carried out, and it redounds to the credit of those who did the work, as well as to the City of Seattle, the possibilities of which were dependent on the great works described.

Not less notable in the making of the city that had the courage to regrade its hills, fill in its tide flats, and build its port was the creation of the Park System. This work was planned and begun while the writer was a member and, part of the time, President of the Park Board. Parkways, now about 60 miles in length, connect the city parks proper and represent a form of regrading of the hills of the city so as to make the beautiful drives which wind about these hills and through much of the primeval forest preserved for the pleasure of future generations. This system is certainly a wonderful creation of man and is the result of allowing full play to the imagination and creative energy of the engineer. Hundreds of thousands will thank the imagination and tireless energy of Mr. Thomson who for more than a score of years was City Engineer and the creator of the future of the City.

Transactions
American Society of Civil Engineers
1926

The "Melting Pot"

Chin Gee Hee, labor capitalist

A Curtis advertising photo: "Blend's Mah Friend"

Keeping Order

Prisoners at McNeil Island Federal Penitentiary (1909)

Detective Agencies——The detective agency is a very important institution in metropolitan life. All of the railroads and other great corporations and many private firms and individuals have constant need of the services of these agencies to keep them informed of their employees, protect them against fraud, and do secret service work in general . . .

Raymer's Dictionary of Greater Seattle
1907

The Naval yard at Bremerton

Since the enthusiastic indorsement (sic) of President McKinley and his policy of expansion at the November election, we hear but few protests against 'imperialism'. The people like it and are not bashful about saying so.

A handful of unbalanced reformers in Massachusetts still shriek and scold and predict revolution, but they are numerically insignificant. As far as the Pacific Coast is concerned, the sentiment is practically unanimous —— in favor of our warlike enterprises in the South Seas.

The Coast
February 1901

Seattle's City Hall, at 3rd and Jefferson, known as "Katzenjammer Castle" because of its numerous alterations and additions.

And within recent years Seattle has been rapidly outgrowing its village stage. The numerous richly-equipped palaces of mammon, the miles of heights embellished with opulent homes, and above all, the hundreds of miles of cement walks and asphalt streets, that have come into existence since 1904, prove that Seattle is really becoming a city of importance. The only damaging evidence that we have not entirely outgrown the wayback City stage of development is to be seen in our so called 'City Hall', which is one of the most extraordinary buildings in America. Hayfork Corners, Arkansas, would be ashamed of such a 'City Hall'. It is a question if Chinese laundrymen would pay rent for quarters in such a building. In short, it is a disreputable, unsanitary old firetrap, of which every public-spirited citizen is heartily ashamed.

The Coast
July 1907

Men of the Labor Temple

Cutting up rhubarb

Women of the Washington Equal Suffrage Association (1910)

'With every copy of 'Votes for Women' goes out a big yellow suffrage poster, different with each issue, which the subscribers are bound by their loyalty to the cause to put up in the most conspicuous spots available. Of this branch of the campaign work, the February number says:

'The poster idea was a great success. From Mannette, Centralia, Walla Walla, Ellensburg, Pullman, and Spokane letters came pouring in telling many tales of putting it up 'after dark', 'on the warehouse on the dock', 'near the church', 'on the way to school', 'on the barn', on the front porch', 'in the front window'. A postmaster's wife hung hers in the post-office, and a grocer's wife hers in the grocery. A woman running a rooming house hung hers in the front hall and a genial boarding house mistress put hers up in the dining room, where it still furnishes the leading topic of conversation. A hostess tacked hers up in the parlor and let it do its duty while she entertained her New Year's callers.'

Collier's
August 1910

Salmon

This packing of fish is as satisfying a pin-money occupation as any industrious woman could wish for. I don't know just how much one of these big canning concerns pays out, in total, for this sort of labor in the course of a fishing season. It depends on the catch. It is piece-work, withal. The wives and daughters of working-men in the neighborhood make from $2.50 to $6.50 a day at it, on the days when the fish come in, and in a good season that is a great many days of the six months. The "high girl" in the Bellingham canneries last year, which was an off-year, cleared up a tidy five hundred dollars in the seventy days on which there were fish to pack, and an Oregon hotel clerk was level-headed and lucky enough to marry her. Women of that spirit and spunk are accorded prizes in new lands. In Bellingham, if you look good and you aren't afraid of getting your hands dirty, the liberal land companies will sell you a plot and build you a tiny bungalow on it on a smaller cash deposit than $500, and there are a lot worse places to be than in Bellingham.

Harper's Weekly
September 1904

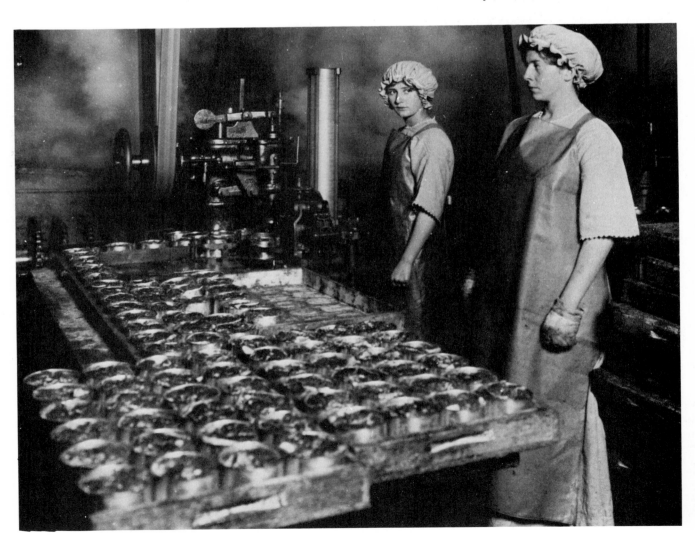

In the Apex Fish Cannery (1913)

Gillnetters waiting the tide at Hole-in-the-wall near La Conner

It is a saying that a man with nothing save an axe and a frying pan can live and live well in the islands of Puget Sound, and there are hundreds of such whose little log houses, or shacks of even a less substantial nature, look out from these shores, which still in many instances are heavily timbered, upon the idyllic beauty of the inland Sea. If they choose to work at all they can find ready occupation at the lumbering or the fishing or any of the other industries that require more muscle than mind . . . This easeful pioneer way of life becomes, they say, an incurable malady. A little work will pay for the bacon, the tea, the sugar and the other small necessities. The woods and the sea provide food in unlimited abundances.

Harper's Weekly
April 1909

Promoting Salmon

Hauling in the nets on a purse seiner

"But some people insist that before long there won't be any fish for anybody to can."

"Well," he said, "that may be true but I don't believe it . . . Personally, I take very little stock in much of the alarmist talk about depletion of the supply. Certainly I do not believe that the fish taken for canning and taken in the traps far out in the salt water are sufficient in number to bring about the annihilation they talk of. Plainly it is to our interests to preserve and perpetuate the supply of fish in every way possible. We have a million and a half dollars invested in this plant and when the fish stop the business stops, but that will be neither in your day nor in mine. My opinion is that that pollution of the water is the thing that will ultimately put an end to the salmon-fishing. The fry will go to sea in billions, but it has been already proven that the fish will not run through sewage and other contaminations to reach a spawning-bed. That is about the only thing that is certain."

Harper's Weekly
September 1904

Timber

In the forest

Sit in the smoking room of any of the steamers that ply up and down the sound and lumber, lumber, lumber is the talk. Big-handed, coarse-bearded loggers, coming to town to blow in their hard-earned summer's wages or off for the camp to saw out more money, fling forth the most wonderful statements of firs that cut forty thousand feet to the tree, and who will look you straight in the eye and tell you that fir is the hardest wood that grows. "Yes, sir--- stronger 'n lots o' cheap wrought iron." They have a lingo all their own and mix it in with Chinook jargon and the weirdest words you ever heard. They talk of one-donkey camps and three-donkey camps, of hook-tenders, of yarders, of fallers and buckers, and by and by you burn to know what these things mean, and to see those giants at work in the woods. Or perhaps you are buttonholed by a lumber king who talks glibly of Chehalis "burns" that will cut so many hundred thousand feet to the acre or of virgin "stands" that cut so many millions. It is all cut, cut, cut, and your civilized horror of the denudation of the forest grows apace.

But once you are set down on the shore of the sound amid the impenetrable jungle, and you see ranchers working their arms off trying to reclaim a few little acres from the wood — see them pulling ten-inch trees up by the roots by a new device worked on the pulley system with the topmost block high up in the hardy giant fir — see them blasting stumps and pecking away at root masses that would defy a Caliban, and are told that in no place has the sound timber been logged off for more than three miles back from the water's edge, while the average is about a mile and a half, and then consider the solemn fact that the big belt runs for hundreds of miles in all directions — you not only lose your urban dread of the denundation of the forest, but actually want to go forth with the saw and axe and do a little denuding yourself. Take the sixty-mile Hood Inlet for example: and there, after a few weeks, you come to long for the sight of a bare strip of earth. For though it has been logged off for a mile back and for long distances up and down shore, the great jungle spreads everywhere. You must not run away with the idea that logging means clearing. It means only the cutting of a big tree here and there, and these only of the best timber. Verily the subduing of the forest has barely been begun in Washington, where the white man found two-thirds of this great corner of the map covered by forest, while along the sound it was all firs, cedars and hemlocks wherever his eye ranged shoreward.

Sunset
November 1909

On the way to market

Beer

Brewing beer

Breweries have already been established at Seattle and elsewhere on Puget Sound, and, as the chief material for beer (barley and hops) are produced here so cheaply and abundantly, we may expect Puget Sound beer to become quite a large item of commerce.

A Report on Washington Territory
1889

Gathering hops in the White River Valley

Perhaps enough of hops might be raised in Washington for the wants of all the world, but it would be impossible to find pickers to handle the crop. Most of the picking is done by Indians, and to this fine, clean, profitable work they come in great numbers in their canoes, old and young, of many different tribes, bringing wives and children and household goods, in some cases from a distance of five or six hundred miles, even from far Alaska. Then they too grow rich and spend their money on red cloth and trinkets. About a thousand Indians are required as pickers at the Snoqualmie ranch alone, and a lively and merry picture they make in the field, arrayed in bright showy calicoes, lowering the rustling vine, pillars with incessant song-singing and fun. Still more striking are their queer camps on the edges of the fields or over on the river bank with the fire-light shining on their wild, jolly faces.

Picturesque California
John Muir

Several years ago almost the entire White River Valley was planted in hops, and it was a curious sight to see the Indian hop pickers every summer. Hops were the great staple product of all the farmers and thousands of dollars were invested in their culture. This, with the rapid growth and development of the nearby metropolis, Seattle, has changed. Now, although many are engaged in raising hops, dairying is the leading occupation.

The Coast
March 1902

Wheat

Plowing sagebrush in Eastern Washington

These raw lands rise quickly in value, and anyone who has the nerve to go out and make a start will in a few years have a good home. The sage brush looks like an impediment —— but the higher the sage the better the soil. Anyone who knows sage brush soil will tell you this. The homesteader, and the man who locates on raw land, will have to live out of a tin can for a few years, and then he will be living in the shade of his own fig tree; for this land develops rapidly. There is little of the discomforts of pioneering which were felt by the men and women who settled the Midwest. The settler in these times can drop into a town in Eastern Washington and a land agent will drive him out in an automobile if he likes. A little capital will go a long way here. Much land is for sale practically without payment. That is, land is for sale on wheat payment plan. So well do the owners of this land know the country that they are willing to sell a piece of land with a small payment down, and take a stated sum each year as the buyer sells his wheat crop.

From a pamphlet of the Adams County
Alaskan-Yukon-Pacific Exhibition
1909

Harvesting wheat in Eastern Washington

What we must do is to make the most of what we have. There should be no restriction on our carrying grain, cotton, steel, machinery, etc. to the Orient. We must give the Japanese and Chinese wheat flour so cheap that they will use it instead of rice. We cannot do that so long as we have not a free hand. You must cut your profits to the very edge to make it possible. We cannot do that so long as we are constantly interfered with. Nor can we do it while the law compels us to tell every tramp steamer captain just what our rates are.

J. J. Hill in
The World's Work
August 1905

The Public Market

The Public Market

Municipal aid to solving the cost of living was begun in Seattle several years ago with the establishment of the Public Market . . . At the first, allowance was made for only a modest beginning, with a small market building and space for a limited number of stalls. The popularity of the project was immediate, the housewife and the truck gardener especially finding satisfaction in the opportunity afforded to deal directly with each other. Not only has the city extended its orginal dimensions, but has established another in a different location, while some similar undertakings are being conducted as private enterprises. In all of these the wares offered for sale and the sanitary conditions are under the supervision of the city's bureau of market inspection.

In the suburbs of Seattle and scattered all about beyond the city limits are innumerable small tracts whose soil is made to yield abundantly in fruits, berries of every kind, and all sorts of vegetables. Near at hand, also, in addition to the big dairy farms and larger creameries, are numerous small dairies of a few good cows and many little chicken ranches. The products of all these, to great extent, are brought directly to the public markets of Seattle...Every day, except Sunday, is market day.

Seattle
The Exploitation and Industrial Bureau of
    the New Seattle Chamber of Commerce
1912

Oysters

Gathering oysters

The oyster industry as yet is in its infancy; but, with the rapid settlement of this Western country and the introduction of the rearing of the Eastern varieties of oysters, it is but fair to presume that this branch of the trade and commercial intercourse will become the most lucrative and interesting. Already, all locations adapted to oyster culture are taken up and held at high figures.. . The largest and most productive beds are located in Hammersley's Inlet, near Shelton in Mason County, and in Oyster Bay, near Camilche on the line dividing Mason and Thurston Counties. In order to further the industry and raise sufficient produce to meet the demands of the fast-increasing trade, men of means have studied the business and invested heavily in artificial methods to increase and force the volume of the bivalve.

The Coast
December 1902

Recreation

A party of mountaineers near Stevens Pass

To the man who wishes to forget, for a few brief days or weeks, the varied occupations that make up his daily life, Puget Sound has many attractions to offer. Whatever ones' ideal may be, he can find it here, whether it is canoeing, rowing, sailing, or cruising in a motor boat, riding, driving, golfing, fishing, motoring, mountain climbing, or just a desire to escape to the wilderness and let nature soak in.

Pacific Monthly
April 1908

The most pressing need in mountain affairs in Washington at the present time is the improvement and extension of the roads of the Mt. Rainier National Park. The mountain is attracting wide attention and people are coming from afar to visit it. If they find the Mountain accessible they will tell their friends about it and the Mountain will receive the best form of publicity. If, on the other hand, they find there are no roads or only fair ones, they will probably so state and by doing so dissuade many from a visit. Now is the time to go at this matter with all the vim that can be shown, and the Mountaineers should be the ones to lead in this work . . .

I realize that the true Mountaineer would much rather see the Mountains from the trail or the unexplored wilderness, but to make mountains at all popular, to get the majority of people in to them, it is necessary to have roads.

The Mountaineer
1911
A. Curtis

One of the objects of the Mountaineer Club is the incultation of a love for nature and a careful observation of her ways; yet it has been remarked that man has usurped the place of nature and become the center of interest. People are interesting at any time, but are especially interesting when thrown in contrast with the things and forces that man is trying to understand and control. Good common-feeling is produced by all reaching the end of a long trail, and by all taking a turn at the snow slide, a closer human kinship is created by attempting to avoid the "squaw-fire" on the supper walks, and by the singing on the long Sound boat ride. This new form of socialization seems to take the place of nature unconsciously, and nature is used rather than enjoyed directly; the elemental habits of walking, eating, swimming, fire-building, singing and the general outdoor life and resulting comraderie are all added bonds that bind the members into closer acquaintance and friendship. That this is the case seems to be indicated by the hazy recollections of the trails traversed, by the constant mingling of all members, by the solicitude envied by all for guests and new members . . .

During the year a new custom has been growing up among the walkers: eating supper in common on the return to the city. From four to thirty-three members have, on several occasions, enjoyed a cafeteria meal together with the usual after-dinner singing. The custom serves as a very practical as well as very pleasant ending to the outing . . .

The Mountaineer
1915

On Mount Rainier

Water Crisis

"More than 150 feet of the main supply pipe of the Cedar River water system was destroyed yesterday when the high water in Cedar River washed out a bridge carrying the pipe across that stream near Landsburg, twenty miles from the city."

"The seriousness of the situation was fully realized this morning when complaints began to pour into the Water Department from private homes, schools and other public buildings.

"A hurried conference was had with Mayor George W. Dilling, and all water wagons owned by the city, some twenty-four in number, and the two electric sprinkling cars, holding 6,000 gallons each, were put into commission. These wagons, drafted from the Street and Park Departments, will be supplied from the low service reservoirs, and will serve that section of the city served by the intermediate service, directly from the Cedar River pipe lines. The sprinkling cars will be run to the Queen Anne Hill and Beacon Hill districts, over the tracks of the Seattle Electric Company."

"This morning the quest for water grew ten thousand fold. Automobiles were driven from fashionable residences on Capitol Hill, in the North Broadway district, on Renton Hill and the Madrona district to the Lincoln Park and Volunteer Park reservoirs. Old and young, men and women, boys and girls, each and all reverted to the primeval instinct of catch for himself or herself."

"Auditor John Lamb of the Water Department issued an order at noon today prohibiting the use of water for bathing purposes. This order extends to public bath houses, apartment houses, clubs and private residences. Any violations of this order, Lamb explained, will result in the cutting off of the water service to the building in which such violation occurs."

Seattle Daily Times
November 20, 1911

Hauling water during the water "famine" (1911)

Education

37773
A.C.

Passing on the culture

About the year nineteen-ten came to me——teacher and spinster——the conviction that fate had paid me the compliment of handing over the reins. She had failed to provide for me that ideal relationship which alone is the basis of the true home, and I was by nature obdurate toward accepting anything less at her hands. When a youthful friend was surreptitiously chidden for using the term "old maid" in my presence, the incident gave rise to thought. What now? I asked myself. *Quo Vadis,* old maid? What will you do with life? . . . For some months, while work went on as usual, I reflected deeply, and gradually evolved the determination to be a creative farmer. There recurred to me the longing and ambition——innate but hitherto suppressed—— to own a portion of the earth's crust in my own right, and to tamper with it unrestrained. I would build a farm, wherein I could exercise my delight in all forms of nature life and to which in time I could bring some unparented little children, on whom to wrack my educational convictions and whom I might hope some day to turn over——a little bunch of good citizens——to my native land.

Homesteader's Portfolio
Alice Day Pratt
1922

Amusements

The young at play

MODEL AIRSHIPS WILL FLY TODAY

Seven Boys Enter Machines in
Last Event of Public
Library Meet

Seven boys are entered in the final event of the first aviation meet ever held on the Pacific Coast which will be held by the public library this afternoon at 3 o'clock at the Lincoln playfield. The previous events were held last week, but owing to lack of competition the prize in class A was not awarded.

The machines which will be flown today must all rise from the ground by their own power, and a runway has been constructed from which to start them.

The first prize is a silver cup, presented by the Bon Marche; second, a silver cup, presented by an aviation enthusiast; third, a miniature tool chest, presented by Spelger & Hurlbut. Herbert Munter, a Seattle aviator, has also promised the winning boy a ride in his aeroplane, providing the consent of the boy's parents is given.

The judges will be Mayor Gill, D. B. Trefethen, of the Library Board, and P.D. Hughes. The meet is held under the auspices of the public library and illustrates one of the many ways used by the library to interest young people in books.

Seattle Post-Intelligencer
September 5, 1914

The beach at Alki Point

Alki Point is the most popular resort near Seattle, being visited by thousands of people every day during the summer. It is located four miles distant across Seattle Harbor and is reached by the staunch little steamers "Dix" and "Manette," which run hourly from the Flyer Dock. At the point there is a long sandy bathing beach, a natorium, summer hotels, bath houses, dancing pavilions, picnic grounds and many other attractive features. It is a most delightful excursion to take a steamer and go there for an hour or two, or for the afternoon and evening, to enjoy the cool breezes blowing in from the Pacific Ocean, to stroll along the beach or into the woods, or to take a plunge into the clear salt water of the Sound.

Every year, several thousand people camp along the shore of the Sound in this vicinity from May until October, and enjoy the pleasures and advantages of the simple life while carrying on their usual business enterprises in the city.

The fare for the round trip is 25 cents.

Where to Go in Seattle and the Puget Sound Country
James Meikle
1905

At the golf club in Laurelhurst

"There is local gossip and small talk a-plenty in the clubs of these Pacific cities, but here big subjects seem larger. You begin to feel that the United States is very much bigger than it seemed in New York. These people have a way, and that without boasting, of assuming that they and not the Eastern people, are the masters of things --- that the ultimate American judgment will be their judgment.

It is difficult to say precisely how they convey this impression. If you talk about politics, they will frankly confess that their politics are bad. Few men of the first-rate ability or of the highest character have time to take an interest in public affairs. If you talk about commerce, the commerce of the Pacific is yet really to be developed. But they do think in large units. You will hear them talk about the effect that the Panama Canal will have, as if the Canal were ten miles from where you are sitting. When they speak of going "South" they mean a pleasure journey of 2,000 miles, more or less, to Southern California. They talk familiarly of tours and camps in Alaska, as if they were a days journey away. They talk of going to New York or Chicago as if they were contiguous cities. Perhaps it is their large units of space that give a sort of continental scope to their thought."

The World's Work
August 1905

Looking up Marion Street from Second Avenue (Seattle): before cars took control of the streets

The frontier is as far removed from them, in fact, as if the city were an old one.

The World's Work
August 1905

The Seattle Symphony

"Seattle . . . will in time become the largest city on the Coast; and, eventually, one of the half-dozen largest in the United States. Why? Because Seattle has within itself all the essentials for the making of a really great city."

No one questions statements so logical and so true in analysis. Materially, Seattle is all that is sprightly and ambitious, shrewd, capable and knowing. Moreover, great institutions for learning have been built, the music of local organizations is liberally patronized, homes are beautified beyond the homes of most other cities away from the Pacific Coast. Yet to the stranger, the sojourner for a week or a month, the City has the cold gloss of a new house in which no fire has yet been lighted; too busy in its rearing, it has no time, so far, to mature a soul. The dollar mark is obstrusively the City's crest. The visitor is greeted with noisy geniality if his pockets jingle hard enough. If his touring car be large and shiny, or if as a "home seeker" he expresses interest in a sightly lot, the eagerness of Seattle is as Californian as ――― Los Angeles.

Given a longer period for the seasoning of its roof-tree, for the mellowing of the wine of courtesy, for the refining of its money-lust, and perhaps we shall have in Seattle a civic personality less brusque, less conscious of its bank clearings, less glib as to the size and cost of its "improvements," a city cultured, not boastful of its literary only, and one more in common with that best of all things — common kindness — unalloyed with self-interest.

The Tourist's Northwest
1916

A Seattle theatre

The Potlatch Parade

Always a hospitable city, and with a welcome waiting for every visitor all the year round, Seattle decided in 1910 that thereafter a week should be set aside each summer during which the whole city should keep open house. The first Potlatch was held in the summer of 1911. The unique name of the celebration, taken from the Chinook jargon, the trade language of the Pacific Coast Indians, meant to the Indians just what it means to Seattle——a period of hospitality, of entertainment, feasting, music, dancing and generally joyous revelry.

The annual Potlatch is under the control of a voluntary association of leading business men and women, but in the past two years the carrying out of details has been wisely left to the Tilikums of Elttaes (Friends of Seattle), an organization of "live wire" citizens, divided into three tribes, whose friendly rivalry for superiority of numbers and attractiveness in Potlatch pageantry keeps local interest at high pitch.

Seattle always decorates in gayest attire for the Potlatch; these are great days for the children, brilliantly illuminated night parades, naval and military displays, automobile and floral parades, daring feats of aviation by world-famous bird-men, and music everywhere. The streets are thronged by day and by night and everyone is happy.

Seattle
The Exploitation and Industrial Bureau of
    the New Seattle Chamber of Commerce
1912

On the Horizon

The streets and public buildings belonging to the City are all lighted now by the recently constructed municipal plant. When the bonds were voted for the construction of this plant, it was generally understood that it was to furnish light and power for all purposes. Every effort has been made, however, by the private corporations engaged in this line of business to prevent the City from supplying light and power to private customers; but, in spite of this opposition, the sale of bonds was recently authorized by an overwhelming popular vote to erect poles and wires for the purpose of distributing light and power for private consumers.. . The voters of the city want cheap light and power and will have little patience with the cry of vested rights raised for the purpose of protecting the profits of the highly capitalized private corporations.

Annals of the American Academy
January 1906

An early service vehicle of City Light

Swooping down from a height of 150 feet and traveling at the rate of forty miles an hour, Charles K. Hamilton lost control of the Curtis biplane in which he was exhibiting at the Meadows yesterday afternoon when he attempted to skim the surface of a small lake inside the race track and was thrown into seven feet of water, his aeroplane turning turtle when it struck.

"It was all the fault of a defective wire attached to one of the planes," said Hamilton . . . " One of the wires was a new one that had been put in just before the exhibition started and it was loose. I attempted to tighten it while I was descending to the water but couldn't do it and of course couldn't steer the machine as I wanted to. When I struck, the water got into the carburetor. This stopped the engine and prevented a recovery, which otherwise might have been made, though I probably was in too deep."

In the first three flights of the afternoon, the daring aviator had won completely the admiration of the crowd and each time after he alighted cheer after cheer echoed and reechoed from the grandstand and all parts of the ground. .

In his first flight Hamilton started on the cinder track near the north entrance to the park, skimming along the ground for 150 feet and then soared gracefully into the air. Twice he circled the track and then descended until he scarcely was fifty feet above the heads of the big crowd at the east end of the race track. After this he made a wide detour to the north, turned south and then east and sank gracefully to the ground in the centre of the field. Not a hand was raised in applause. Not a cheer greeted him. But it was not because his feat was not appreciated. The crowd was as if in a trance. It was Seattle's first glimpse of the most modern aerial navigation, and for a few minutes the crowd was so filled with awe that they could not express their feelings. . . After that they were less prepared for the sight that met their eyes on the fourth flight when he dashed into the water. He had become a hero in their eyes, a man that did things, and when they thought that he was conquered by water after such a successful conquest of the air, they were ready to grieve as for a friend, through they had known him but two hours, and at an average distance of a quarter of a mile.

The Seattle Sunday Times
March 13, 1910

C. K. Hamilton bringing the plane to Seattle

Learning About Puget Sound Past

Regional history, unfortunately, is often an exercise in self-glorification. National and global history is not too much different, but in local history we find the most obvious odes to the founding fathers. Do not be put off by the snobbish aspects, but persevere. The history of a small area contains the same drama and pathos as does History, on the larger world stage.

The best way to learn about the past is to talk to people who lived there, (though the limitations of this technique are obvious). Such people are not to be found in one spot but are scattered throughout; you are your own best guide to finding them.

The next best way to get a sense of the past is to browse through the "working papers" of a particular period: magazines, newspapers, books, pamphlets, letters, diaries, journals, photographs, maps, posters, and guidebooks. Printers wasted no time in coming to Washington Territory, so you have much to choose from in formal material.

Letters, diaries, journals: The papers of only the most famous people are honored by publication. However, less noted people often had fascinating lives, and their papers often repose in unjustified quiet but are available for your perusal. Do not be frivolous; most librarians rightfully view such primary sources as gold and will prevent your access unless you seem correctly respectful.

Periodicals: Our major libraries have enormous collections which are constantly growing as present becomes past. Go in and browse through issues (chosen at random or around a famous event) of the daily or weekly newspapers (e.g. Seattle Daily Times, Post-Intelligencer, Star, etc.) or issues of regional magazines such as The Argus, The Coast, Pacific Monthly, or Sunset. National magazines such as Harper's Weekly, Collier's or the National Geographic are interesting, too.

Pamphlets: Like graffiti, pamphlets and other odd printed numbers are often so commonplace that no one bothered to collect them. They are rich but might only be found bound together with others related to the same topic.

Guidebooks: **The Last Whole Earth Catalog** and **Europe On $5 A Day** are only the latest in an old American tradition of books designed to provide useful information. The guidebooks went along with the settling of the West: for example, the process of obtaining land

under the Homestead Act would be explained. Practical information indeed! Even today they are useful as they provide insights into daily life that are often too trivial for standard historians to note.

Secondary sources: The following titles are good reading.

Meany, Edmond S. **Origin of Washington Geographic Names,** Detroit, Michigan. Gale Research Co., 1968. Reprint of 1923 edition.

Meinig, Donald W. **The Great Columbia Plain: A Historical Geography, 1805 - 1910.** University of Washington Press. 1968

American Friends Service Committee. **Uncommon Controversy: Fishing Rights of the Muckleshoot, Puyallup, and Nisqually Indians.** University of Washington Press. 1970

Bacon, George H. **Booming and Panicking on Puget Sound.** Bellingham, Whatcom Museum of History and Art, 1970

Morgan, Murray. **Skid Road: An Informal Portrait of Seattle.** Ballantine Books, 1971

Carey, Roland. **The Sound and the Mountain.** Seattle. Alderbrook Publishing Co., 1970

Newell, Gordon R. **The Green Years: The Development of Transportation, Trade and Finance in the Puget Sound Region from 1886 to 1969 As Recalled by Joshua Green.** Superior, 1969

Clark, Norman H. **Mill Town: A Social History of Everett, Washington from Its Earliest Beginning on the Shores of Puget Sound to the Tragic and Infamous Event Known as the Everett Massacre.** University of Washington Press. 1970

Mills, Hazel, ed. **Read About Washington State: A Selected List of Books Published During 1958 - 1971** Olympia, Washington State Library, 1972

Some bookstores, such as Shorey's in Seattle, can provide reprints of historical documents or may even have issues of old periodicals available. Of course, the Washington State Historical Society in Tacoma and the Pacific Northwest Collection at the University of Washington in Seattle have superb sources. But do not ignore your local or regional library or historical society.

Historical Societies and Museums

Adams County Historical Society
Ritzville, Washington 99169

Adam East Museum
604 S. Ironwood Drive
Moses Lake, Washington 98837

Asotin County Historical Society
Clarkston, Washington 99403

Benton County Museum & Historical Society
Museum Board Chairman & Curator
Prosser, Washington 99350

Camp 6 (Junior League)
3223 Olympic Blvd.
Tacoma, Washington

Chelan County Historical Society
Sunset Highway
Cashmere, Washington 98815

Clallam County Historical Society
Route 3, Box 472
Sequim, Washington 98382

Cowlitz County Historical Society
824 Bebe Road
Castle Rock, Washington 98611

Douglas County Historical Society
P. O. Box 303
Waterville, Washington 98850

Eastern Washington State Historical Society
2316 West First Avenue
Spokane, Washington 99204

Fort Simcoe at Mool—Mool Restoration Society
1120 Larson Building
Yakima, Washington 98901

Fort Vancouver Historical Society
P. O. Box 1834
Vancouver, Washington 98663

Fox Island Historical Society
P. O. Box 54
Fox Island, Washington 98333

Franklin County Historical Society
P. O. Box 1033
Pasco, Washington 99301

Grant County Historical Society
529 D Street, S.W.
Ephrata, Washington 98823

Grays Harbor Historical Association
308 West 6th Street
Aberdeen, Washington 98520

Island County Historical Society
P. O. Box 184
Coupeville, Washington

Jefferson County Historical Society
City Hall
Port Townsend, Washington 98368

Kitsap County Historical Society, Inc.
837 Fourth Street
Bremerton, Washington 98310

Kittitas County Historical Society
1006 East Seattle Avenue
Ellensburg, Washington 98926

Klickitat County Historical Society
P. O. Box 306A
Goldendale, Washington 98620

Lewis County Historical Society
722 Euclid Way
Centralia, Washington 98531

Lincoln County Historical Society
P. O. Box 585
Davenport, Washington 99122

Lopez Island Historical Society
P. O. Box 78
Lopez, Washington 98261

McCleary Historical Society
P. O. Box 194
McCleary, Washington 98557

Mason County Historical Society
Route 3, Box 15
Belfair, Washington 98528

Mukilteo Historical Society, Inc.
Box 166
Mukilteo, Washington 98275

North Central Washington Museum
2 South Chelan Street
Wenatchee, Washington 98801

North Mason Historical Society
North Shore Road
Belfair, Washington 98528

Okanogan County Historical Society
P. O. Box 553
Omak, Washington 98841

Orcas Island Historical Society
Route 1, Box 15A
Eastsound, Washington 98245

Owen Pioneer Museum
Pacific County Historical Society
Ocean Park, Washington 98640

Pend Oreille County Historical Society
Route 1, Box 28
Bickleton, Washington 99322

Peninsula Historical Society
Route 6, Box 6183
Gig Harbor, Washington 98335

Renton Historical Society
1326 Kennewick N.E.
Renton, Washington 98055

San Juan Historical Society
P. O. Box 217
Friday Harbor, Washington 98250

Seattle Historical Society
2161 E. Hamlin Street
Seattle, Washington 98102

Shaw Island Library & Historical Society
Shaw Island, Washington 98286

Skagit County Historical Society
P. O. Box 424
Mount Vernon, Washington 98273

Skamania County Historical Society
Route 1, Box 600
Washougal, Washington 98671

Snohomish County Museum & Historical Assoc.
201 Alverson Blvd.
Everett, Washington 98201

Snoqualmie Valley Historical Society
P. O. Box 179
North Bend, Washington 98045

State Capitol Historical Association
211 W. 21st Avenue
Olympia, Washington 98501

Steilacoom Historical Museum Association
P. O. Box 16
Steilacoom, Washington 98388

Stevens County Historical Society
Addy, Washington 99101

Thomas Burke Memorial Museum
University of Washington
Seattle, Washington 98195

Wahkiakum County Historical Society
Route 1
Cathlamet, Washington 98612

Walla Walla Valley Pioneer & Historical Society
P. O. Box 1616
Walla Walla, Washington 99362

Whatcom County Historical Society
2411 Grant Street
Bellingham, Washington 98225

White River Valley Historical Society
610 Clark Street
Kent, Washington 98031

Yakima Valley Museum & Historical Association
3105 Tieton Drive
Yakima, Washington 98902

Afterword

"Don't look back," Satchel Paige once said, "somebody may be gaining on you." Today Seattle is looking back, and something is gaining on us. It is an awareness and appreciation of the rich, colorful history of our city. From people-filled places like Pioneer Square and the Pike Place Market, to packets of yellow edged photographs tucked away in drawers in quiet museums, the past is being reborn.

Of course, part of this interest is based on curiosity. We want to know how Seattle made the transition from tree covered hills to a concentrated urban center. Part is based on amusement. It's fun to look at the styles of dress, the merchandise, and the primitive industry of previous years. But there is more.

A very large part of our interest in the past comes from a growing recognition that there are things of great value for us there, if we will only take the time to see them. We have come full circle in our respect for such things as public transportation; personal craftsmanship; and the natural beauty of the land which Man cannot duplicate, no matter how great his vision, or how refined his technology.

These are but a few of the qualities of our life which we lost during the intense periods of change which were recorded by Asahel Curtis. These were the times of transition for Seattle, the advent of the automobile, the land tract developments, the smoke belching factories and the multistoried buildings that Seattle saw as its passports to the twentieth century. Curtis used his camera to glorify these changes; but today his pictures also stand as an indictment of our greed, opportunism, and lack of foresight. Yet they also are a monument to his genius, because he did the impossible; he captured rapid change on still photographs that both pinpoint the history of technology, and are timeless in their vision of humanity.

Seattle has a great deal to learn from these pictures of the past. We should admire the men and women who built our city and respect their courage, their tenacity, and the scope of their dreams. But never again should we allow ourselves to succumb to the complete passion for progress which inspired them.

Growth is no longer an absolute good, for which all else is sacrificed. Seattle still must grow, change, and evolve. But we must do so in ways that are controlled, and with full awareness of the consequences. At times, the decision *not* to build, *not* to expand, *not* to change, may be the truest sign of the progress of our maturity.

History, with its triumphs and its mistakes, is a lesson available for all of us to read. As Santayana has said: "Those who do not remember the past are condemned to repeat it." If we are wise enough to profit by it, perhaps we may succeed in reliving some of its joys and avoiding some of its errors as we make history of our own for future generations.

Wes Uhlman

Murray Morgan is a reporter, author and historian.

David Sucher is an environmental planner.

Wes Uhlman is Mayor of Seattle.